Welcome to and Table Talk

Exploring the Bible together to discover the Real Jesus

XTB stands for **eXplore The Bible**.

Read a bit of the Bible each day.

Zoom in on the seven signposts.

Discover who Jesus is and why He came.

Are you ready to explore the Bible? Fill in the bookmark...

...then turn over the page to start exploring with XTB!

Table Talk FOR FAMILIES

Table Talk helps children and adults explore the Bible together.

It can used by:

- Families
- One adult with one child
- Children's leaders with their groups
- Any other way you want to try

Table Talk uses the same Bible passages as XTB so that they can be used together if wanted. Table Talk is enclosed at the back of this book. It's easy to spot because it's printed sideways!

Never done anything like this before? Check our web page for some further help (www.thegoodbook.co.uk/daily_reading/xtb.htm) or write in for a fact sheet.

Sometimes I'm called

Veever the beever (nickname)

My birthday is

February 27th 2007

My age is

9 years old

The best bit about summer is

Spending times with people

OLD TESTAMENT	NEW TESTAMENT
Genesis	Matthew
Exodus	Mark
Leviticus	Luke
Numbers	John
Deuteronomy	Acts
Joshua	Romans
Judges	1 Corinthians
Ruth	2 Corinthians
1 Samuel	Galatians
2 Samuel	Ephesians
1 Kings	Philippians
2 Kings	Colossians
1 Chronicles	1 Thessalonians
2 Chronicles	2 Thessalonians
Ezra	1 Timothy
Nehemiah	2 Timothy
Esther	Titus
Job	Philemon
Psalms	Hebrews
Proverbs	James
Ecclesiastes	1 Peter
Song of Solomon	2 Peter
Isaiah	1 John
Jeremiah	2 John
Lamentations	3 John
Ezekiel	Jude
Daniel	Revelation
Hosea	
Joel	
Amos	
Obadiah	
Jonah	
Micah	
Nahum	
Habakkuk	
Zephaniah	
Haggai	
Zechariah	
Malachi	

How to find your way around the Bible.

**Look out for the READ sign.
It tells you what Bible bit to read.**

READ
John 20v30

**So, if the notes say... READ John 20v30
...this means chapter 20 and verse 30
...and this is how you find it.**

Use the **Contents** page in your Bible to find
where John begins

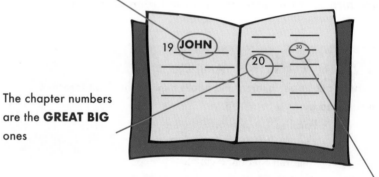

The chapter numbers
are the **GREAT BIG**
ones

The verse numbers are the
tiny ones!

**Oops! Keep getting lost?
Cut out this bookmark and use it to keep your place.**

How to use xtb

1 Find a time and place when you can read the Bible each day.

2 Get your Bible, a pencil and your XTB notes.

3 Ask God to help you to understand what you read.

4 Read today's XTB page and Bible bit.

5 Pray about what you have read and learned.

6 If you can, talk to an adult about what you've learned. Remind them about **Table Talk** at the back of this booklet.

YOUR FREE MAGNIFYING GLASS

Summer Signposts comes with a free magnifying glass. You'll need it to spot the clues, check your puzzles and spy out the signposts. It's handy for keeping an eye on escaping stick insects too!

Do you lose stuff easily? Keep your magnifier in the plastic pocket on the front of this book. Or make a small hole in the plastic pocket, tie some string or wool to it, and hang it somewhere you'll be able to find it later. **Not** on the dog!

Are you ready to spot your first summer signpost? Then hurry on to Day 1.

DAY 1 — SIGN LANGUAGE

Welcome to John's Gospel. It's one of four books—Matthew, Mark, Luke and John—called **Gospels**.

Use your magnifying glass to see what "Gospel" means.

The four Gospels tell us the Good News about **who** Jesus is and **why** He came. Read today's verses to find out why John wrote his Gospel...

John is saying that miracles are like signposts. *Use your magnifying glass again to see what the miracles point to.*

The miracles point us to who Jesus is, so that we can believe in Him, and have everlasting life with God.

READ
John 20v30-31

Why did John write his book?
(*Fill in the gaps*)

> "so that you may **b**_elieve_
> that **J**_esus_ is the Christ
> (Messiah), the **S**_on_ of **G**_od_ ,
> and that by believing you may have
> **l**_ife_ in His name." (v31)

Did You Know?
John's dad was called Zebedee!

Summer Signposts will help you to find out more about what this means.

PRAY — **Dear God, please help me to learn more about Jesus as I read John's book. Amen**

WINE SIGN

Do you remember what John said about miracles?

Miracles point to who Jesus is...

...so that we can believe in Him.

As you read about Jesus' first miracle, think carefully about these two questions:

1 What **miracle** did Jesus do?

2 Who **believed** in Jesus after seeing this miracle?

READ
John 2v1-11

The answers to the questions are hidden in the water jars.

Circle the **two** correct answers.

Did you know?

Jewish wedding parties could last a week—or even longer!

This was Jesus' first miracle. It pointed to who He really is. It showed His glory—how great He is. What did the disciples do? (v11)

They... believed in Jesus from then on.

The disciples DIDN'T understand everything about Jesus. *Do you?*

THINK + PRAY

The disciples DID believe in Jesus. *Do you?*

Talk to God about your answers. Ask Him for help.

Answers: Jars C and E

THE ONE O'CLOCK MIRACLE

John 4v46-54

Yesterday's miracle happened at a happy event—a party. Today's story starts in the same town—Cana. But the man we meet comes from 20 miles away, in Capernaum, and he isn't happy at all. He's really worried because his son is very ill...

READ
John 4v46-54

Our XTB artist is called Kirsty. Usually she draws great pictures —but she hasn't finished these ones! Can you fill in the missing bits?

How do you think the father felt, as he hurried home to see his son?
(Circle) your answers, and add some more.

worried   scared

hopeful   trusting

THINK + PRAY

Read verse 50 again.
The father didn't wait for proof. He took Jesus at His word. That's what faith is. Faith isn't a feeling. It means **believing** that what God says in the Bible is true.

Do YOU believe God's words in the Bible?

YES
Faith is a gift from God. Thank Him for helping you to believe.

NOT SURE
Ask God to help you to believe.

DAY 4 ✓ MAT MATTERS

READ
John 5v1-9

Circle the right words:

The pool was near the **Sheep**/Camel/Dung Gate. It had 4/**5**/6 porches. A great number of people lay by the pool, hoping to **get better**/get wet/get a sun tan. One man had been ill for 28/**38**/48 years. Jesus asked him, "Do you need/care/**want** to get well?" The man replied, "When I'm trying to get in to the pool, someone else **gets there first**/drains the pool/laughs at me." Jesus said, "Get up! Pick up your hockey stick/hammer/**mat** and walk." The man was cured the next day/ **that afternoon**/at once. The day this happened was the **Sabbath**/Tuesday/Christmas Day.

This man was walking for the first time in 38 years! What would **you** say to him?

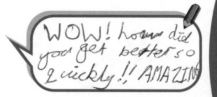

WOW! how did you get better so quickly!! AMAZING

Read Verse 10 to find out what some people actually said to the man.
✔ *Tick the correct speech bubble.*

Wow—you can walk! That's great!

Who healed you? He must be very special.

Stop that! It's against the rules! ✔

Those Jewish leaders completely missed the point! (*More about them tomorrow.*)

THINK SPOT

Imagine being told to walk if you hadn't moved your legs for 38 years! It sounds crazy! What would YOU have done?

This man obeyed Jesus—and was healed. Sometimes obeying Jesus is hard —or seems silly—but John's book will help us to see why **OBEYING JESUS IS ALWAYS THE BEST THING TO DO.**

PRAY

Dear Jesus, please help me to obey You, even when I find it hard. Amen

MISSING THE POINT

READ
John 5v9-15

The Jewish leaders made rules about the **Sabbath** (God's special day of rest). One rule was...

SABBATH
RULE

You mustn't carry anything!

Draw yourself here. How do **you** react to Jesus? Talk to God about your answer.

WORD POOL
Use these words to fill in the gaps

pleased cross kill believe hated obeyed

Choose words from the word pool
Were they:
• p_leased_ because the man was well? ✔ or ✗
• or c_ross_ because he was carrying his mat? ✔ or ✗

We've seen **two** very different reactions to Jesus:
1. The man o_beys_ Jesus.
2. The Jewish leaders h_ates_ Jesus.

READ
John 5v16-18

They
didn't b_elieve_ Jesus was God's Son. They thought He was lying, and planned to k_ill_ Him (v18).

Now the Jewish leaders were **furious!** *Draw their faces.*

FISHY BUSINESS

John
6v5-13

Everywhere Jesus went, crowds of people came to see Him. One day a huge and hungry crowd followed Jesus up a hill...

Write these answers in the five loaves.

5 ~~12~~ ~~5000~~
~~2~~ ✗

READ
John 6v5-13

How many loaves? — 5

How many men? — 5000

How many fish? — 2

How many baskets? — 12

How many people could have done this? — 1

Did You know? They only counted **men** in the crowd. If you add the women and children, Jesus probably fed over 15,000 people!

Only **one** person could do a miracle like this—**JESUS**.

Wow!

THINK + PRAY

Sometimes we may think that we have problems that are impossible to solve: they're just TOO BIG. What's your biggest problem at the moment?

_____

Remember: even the biggest problem is NO PROBLEM for Jesus. Ask Him to help you.

DAY 7 — IF THE HAT FITS... ✓

xtb — John 6v14-15

Historical Hat Quiz

more answers hidden in text!

Which army had taken control of Israel at the time of Jesus?

The Roman army

What were the people in Israel waiting for God to do?

Send a king to rescue them

What's this got to do with Jesus feeding a huge crowd with one boy's packed lunch?

Send the verses to find out

READ
John 6v14-15

What did the crowds want Jesus to become?

KING

Jesus was their King ✓

The crowds were RIGHT but they were WRONG!

He hadn't come to get rid of the Romans ✗

Jesus the King DID come to rescue His people—but NOT by freeing them from the Romans. *We'll find out more about how Jesus rescues people on Day 14.*

Christians are people who follow Jesus as their King, doing what He wants them to do. Jesus is in charge.

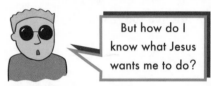

But how do I know what Jesus wants me to do?

What would you say to Simon?

Talk to ~~Siuq~~ friends and read the bible to understa...

Clue: Mention the Bible and older Christians.

PRAY

What day is it today?
Wednesday

King Jesus, please help me to obey You today and every day. Amen

WALKING ON WHAT! ER?

John 6v16-21

What are you scared of...?
(✔ the boxes)

spiders

snakes

thunder & lightning

the dark

In today's story, the disciples are in a boat on a dark, stormy night. But it's not the storm they're scared of—it's **Jesus!**

READ
John 6v16-21

Check out the five miracles John has told us about so far...

1 2 3

4 5

What do these miracles all show about Jesus? (*Fill in a, e, i, o, u*)

Jesus Is the Christ, the Son of God.
You can check your answer in John 20v31 (Day 1)

Read verse 20 again.

Did you know?

The most often repeated command in the Bible is "Don't be afraid". Repeated 366 times. One for each day of the year, and one extra in case you have a particularly scary day!

THINK + PRAY

Think again about WHO Jesus is. Why should that help you not to be afraid?

Jesus is ALWAYS able to help us—and He NEVER lets us down. Thank Jesus for being like this.

SIGHT FOR SORE EYES

Find the tiniest thing in the room—and look at it through the magnifying glass. What did you look at? a crums

The man in today's story couldn't see tiny things—or **HUGE** stuff. He was born blind. It's a l-o-n-g story. We'll *zoom in* on three snapshots—but if you can, read the whole of chapter 9 first.

READ
John 9v6-9

Jesus healed the man with the world's first mud pack! *Fill in what people said:*

> Isn't this the blind man who used to sit and b eg ? (v8)

> No, he only l ooks like him! (v9)

The Pharisees (Jewish leaders) didn't believe it either—so they asked his mum and dad!

READ
John 9v18-21

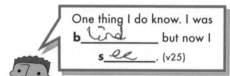

> We know he is our s on (v20)

> We know he was b orn b lind (v20)

But the Pharisees **still** didn't believe it. They were sure Jesus couldn't be from God, so they quizzed the man again...

READ
John 9v24-25

> One thing I do know. I was b lind but now I s ee . (v25)

This man didn't know everything about Jesus. But he spoke up about the things he DID know. How about YOU? What could you tell somebody else about Jesus?

THINK + PRAY

WHO could you tell about Jesus this week?

Thomas

Ask God to help you.

WHAT AN EYE-OPENER!

Look at the picture. What do you see?

Do you see a vase? Or two people talking? *(You may need help to see both.)*

The man in yesterday's story was born **b l i n d**. Did you know that **you** were born **b l i n d** too? It's true! Everyone is born *spiritually blind*. That means we can't see **who** Jesus really is. We need help.

READ
John 9v35-38

This man's eyes were now fully open.

His **physical** eyes could see

His **spiritual** eyes could see

Arrow Code

A = ⇧
D = ⇩
E = ⇩
F = ⬈
G = ⇦
H = ⬋
L = ➘
M = ⬇
N = ↗
O = ⬅
P = ⬉
R = ◁
T = ◁

Crack the code to see how his understanding of Jesus grew.

First he just called Jesus a M A N

Then a P R O P H E T

Then he saw Jesus was from G O D

Finally he called Jesus his L O R D

As you grow up there'll be loads to learn—about maths, computers or how to draw camels! But the most important thing is to keep learning about **Jesus**.

THINK + PRAY

Do you want to know Jesus better, and understand what the Bible says about Him? If so, you need to ask for His help. Ask Jesus to open your eyes, so that you can come to know Him better and better.

DAY 11 — DYING TO SEE YOU

Joe's friends **hadn't** forgotten him—they had something better planned.

READ
John 11v1-3

Lazarus was **dying**. What do you think Jesus did when He heard the news?
a) Rushed off to see Lazarus at once.
b) Healed Lazarus immediately from where He was.
c) Stayed where He was for 2 more days.

READ
John 11v4-6

The answer is c) Jesus stayed put for two more days! How odd! Why did Jesus say this had happened? (v4)

It is for God's **g**lory so that the **S**on of God may be glorified through it.

Later, Jesus said something even more astonishing...

Lazarus is dead, and for your sake I am glad I was not there. (v14-15)

WHY??

 xtb   John 11v1-6

At this point in the story the disciples don't understand why Jesus has waited. Later they would see that Jesus had something better planned.

We'll find out more tomorrow.

THINK + PRAY

Do you ever pray about something that's really important to you—and nothing seems to happen? Don't give up! God NEVER ignores your prayers. But sometimes He has something better planned. Ask God to help you to trust Him—and to wait for His answer.

DAY 12 # LIFE OR DEATH

 John 11v17-27

Mary and Martha had sent a message to Jesus to tell Him that their brother Lazarus was dying. But Jesus waited **two days** before going to them. When He got there, Lazarus was dead...

READ
John 11v17-22

How long had Lazarus been dead? (v17)

__2__ days

Martha believed that Jesus could have saved her brother. But now Jesus told her something even more amazing...

READ
John 11v23-27

Did you know?

Risen • Raised • Resurrection
These words all mean a dead person coming back to life.

Did you find verse 25 hard to understand? *Use these words to complete the XTB Xplanation Xtra:*

Jesus **life**

XTB XPLANATION XTRA

J _esus_ is the resurrection and the l _ife_ . This means that J _esus_ will bring back to l _ife_ everyone who believes in Him. They will have eternal l _ife_ with J _esus_ in heaven.

Life on earth **ends**. Life with Jesus in heaven **never ends!**

THINK SPOT

Do you worry about dying? Everyone dies. But if we believe in Jesus we don't need to be scared of dying. We know that we will be with Him in heaven for ever.

PRAY **Thank You Jesus that You came to rescue everyone who believes in You. Amen**

DEAD OR ALIVE?

Lazarus had been dead for **four days**. His tomb was a cave, sealed with a huge stone. Jesus went there with Mary and Martha.

READ
John 11v32-37

Mary believed that Jesus could have healed her brother—but look at what some other people said.

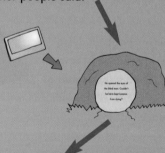

He opened the eyes of the blind man. Couldn't he have kept Lazarus from dying?

The answer is **YES!!!**
—but Jesus was about to do something even more amazing!

READ
John 11v38-45

Jesus had the stone moved, and then ordered Lazarus to come out. What happened? (v44)

He came out wrapped in cloths and with a towel around his face.

Imagine how **stunned** people were to see Lazarus walk out of the tomb! How many of them believed in Jesus? (v45)

Circle the correct answer on the open tomb.

 THINK SPOT

Many people believed in Jesus after seeing this amazing miracle. What about you? Have YOU put your faith in Jesus?

NOT YET

(If you're not sure, tomorrow's reading will help you.)

THINK + PRAY

John wrote about these seven miracles to help us to see clearly who Jesus is and to believe in Him. *Have they helped you to believe in Jesus? Do they help you to trust Jesus when things are hard?* **Talk to God about your answers.**

DAY 14 — WHY DID JESUS COME?

John has written about **seven** miracles. Can you put them in the correct order? (*Answers at the bottom of the page.*)

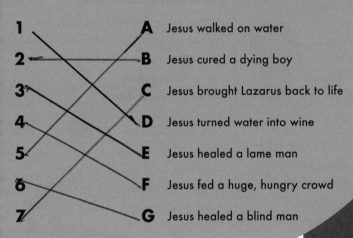

1
2
3
4
5
6
7

A Jesus walked on water

B Jesus cured a dying boy

C Jesus brought Lazarus back to life

D Jesus turned water into wine

E Jesus healed a lame man

F Jesus fed a huge, hungry crowd

G Jesus healed a blind man

These miracles are like **seven signposts**. What do they point to?

John has shown us **who** Jesus is. Now we're going to find out **why** Jesus came...

READ
John 3v16

• **Who** sent Jesus into the world?   G_od_

• **Why** did God send Jesus?   because He _loves_ us.

God's everlasting love for us is the reason He sent Jesus. To find out more read **God's Rescue Plan** on the next page.

PRAY

Father God, thank you that You love me so much that You sent Jesus to rescue me. Amen

GOD'S RESCUE PLAN

Why did God rescue us—and **who** is the Rescuer? John 3v16 explains it.

For God loved the world so much...

This is the reason for the Rescue Plan. God's **everlasting love** for you and me. He wants us to know Him and to be His friends. But there's a problem. SIN gets in the way.

What is Sin?

We all like to be in charge of our own lives. We do what **we** want instead of what **God** wants. This is called Sin.

Sin gets in the way between us and God. It stops us from knowing Him and stops us from being His friends. The final result of sin is death. You can see why we need to be rescued!

...that He gave His only Son...

God sent Jesus to be our Rescuer—to save us from the problem of sin.

How did Jesus rescue us?

At the first Easter, when Jesus was about 33 years old, He was crucified. He was nailed to a cross and left to die.

As He died, all the sins of the world (all the wrongs people had done) were put onto Jesus. He took all of our sin onto Himself, taking the punishment we deserve. He died in our place, as our Rescuer, so that we can be forgiven.

...so that everyone who believes in Him may not die but have eternal life. (*John 3v16*)

When Jesus died He dealt with the problem of sin. That means that there is nothing to separate us from God any more. That's great news for you and me!

We can know God today as our Friend and King—and one day live in heaven with Him for ever.

Have YOU been rescued by Jesus? Turn to the next page to find out more...

Did you know?

Jesus died on the cross as our Rescuer—but He didn't stay dead! After three days God brought Him back to life! Jesus is still alive today, ruling as our King.

AM I A CHRISTIAN?

Not sure if you're a Christian? Then check it out below...

Christians are people who have been rescued by Jesus and follow Him as their King.

> You can't become a Christian by trying to be good.

That's great news, since you can't be totally good all the time!

It's about accepting what Jesus did on the cross to rescue you. To do that, you will need to **ABCD**.

A **Admit** your sin—that you do, say and think wrong things. Tell God you are sorry. Ask Him to forgive you, and to help you to change. There will be some wrong things you have to stop doing.

B **Believe** that Jesus died for you, to take the punishment for your sin; that He came back to life, and that He is still alive today.

C **Consider** the cost of living like God's friend from now on, with Him in charge. It won't be easy. Ask God to help you do this.

D **Do** something about it! In the past you've gone your own way rather than God's way. Will you hand control of your life over to Him from now on? If you're ready to ABCD, then talk to God now. The prayer will help you.

> Dear God,
> I have done and said and thought things that are wrong. I am really sorry. Please forgive me. Thank you for sending Jesus to die for me. From now on, please help me to live as one of Your friends, with You in charge.   Amen

> Do you remember Jesus' promise?—"everyone who believes in Him shall not die but have eternal life." John 3v16

Jesus welcomes everyone who comes to Him. If you have put your trust in Him, He has rescued you from your sins and will help you to live for Him. That's great news!

WICKED PLOT OR WONDERFUL PLAN?

xtb John 19v23-27

WICKED PLOT

The more miracles Jesus did, the more His enemies plotted to kill Him. In the end they arrested Jesus, and handed Him over to the Romans.

The Roman Governor—*Pontius Pilate*—agreed to have Jesus crucified. Jesus was nailed to a cross, and left to die. Two other men were put to death at the same time.

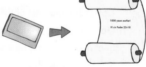

The **Wicked Plot** seemed to have won. **BUT** (as we saw yesterday) it was really all part of God's **Wonderful Plan** to rescue us...

WONDERFUL PLAN

READ
John 19v23-27

What an awful thing to do: taking the clothes of a dying man. **BUT** check the scroll to see **how long ago** God had said this would happen!

Jesus was in agony—**BUT** that didn't stop Him caring for His mother and making sure she would be looked after.

♥ **JESUS LOVED MARY**
(*He asked John to care for her.*)

♥ **HE DIED TO SAVE EVERYONE**
(*Jesus died because He loves us and came to rescue us.*)

Find all the blue words in the wordsearch.

HE ♥ TO
DIEDMARY
JESUSLOVED
EVERYONE
SAVE
ME

What word is left over? __ME__
Add it to the prayer.

PRAY Thank you Jesus for loving __ME__ so much that You died for me. Amen

DAY 16 **ALL FINISHED**

I've finished!

Tom and Sally have **finished** what they planned to do. In today's verses Jesus **finishes** what He has come to do...

READ
John 19v28-30

Why did Jesus ask for a drink? (v28)

▷ ⇨ ◁ ↑ ↖ ◁ ▽ ◁ ⇩

So that __ __ __ __ __ __ __ __ __ __ __

◁ ◁ ▽ ⇩

would come __ __ __ __

Jesus knew He was completing the Rescue Plan that God had spoken of in Scripture (the oldest part of the Bible).

Arrow Code

C = ⇨
D = ⬈
E = ⇩
I = ↑
J = ↗
O = ⬅
P = ↖
R = ◁
S = ▷
T = ◁
U = ▽

Crack the code to find out what Jesus had finished.

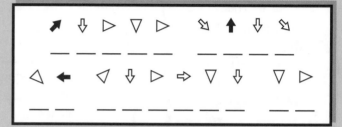

↗ ⇩ ▷ ▽ ▷ ⬈ ↑ ⇩ ⬈
__ __ __ __ __ __ __ __ __

◁ ⬅ ◁ ⇩ ▷ ⇨ ▽ ⇩ ▽ ▷
__ __ __ __ __ __ __ __ __ __

As Jesus died **all** the sins of the world (all the wrongs people had done) were put onto Him. He took **all** of our sin onto Himself, taking **all** the punishment we deserve. There was nothing else Jesus had to do to rescue us. His job as our Rescuer was **finished**.

THINK + PRAY

The day Jesus died is called **Good Friday.** That's because Jesus did a **good** thing when He rescued us from our sins. **Thank God for sending Jesus to rescue you.**

THE END OF THE ROAD?

It's Friday afternoon—and Jesus is dead. His body must be moved before sunset, when the Sabbath begins.

The Roman soldiers check first, to make sure that Jesus really is dead.

Then two of Jesus' followers ask Pilate, the Roman Governor, if they can have the body.

They put s_____ on the body, and wrap it in strips of l_____ cloth. (v40)

Jesus is buried by J_____ (from Arimathea) and N_____

READ
John 19v38-42

Then they bury Jesus in a n_____ tomb, and seal it with a huge stone. (v41)

Is this the end of the road?

Dear God, thank you that You are always in control. Please help me to trust You.

But God was **always** in control. God's wonderful rescue plan is about to win in an amazing way!

Jesus is dead and buried. It **looks** like the wicked murder plot has won.

DAY 18

RUN AND SEE

1 When you race with your friends, do you usually come **first**, **last** or somewhere in the **middle**?

READ
John 20v1-8

When Mary found that Jesus' body was missing, she thought grave robbers had pinched it. She ran to tell Peter and John. They raced off to see for themselves.

2 Who got to the tomb first? (v4) **J_____**

Who was first to go right inside? (v6) **P_____**

What did they see?

Grave robbers would never leave the valuable linen cloth behind! Something else must be going on...

3
READ
John 20v9

The **Scriptures** (the oldest part of the Bible) said that Jesus would come back to life again.

Jesus had said so as well. (*You can read His words in Luke 18v31-34*)

But Jesus' friends **hadn't understood**.

BUT Now John had seen the empty tomb for himself—with the grave-clothes still lying there. What did he do?

He saw and b_____ (v8)

4

- Like Jesus' friends, do you sometimes find it hard to **understand** what God is telling you in the Bible?
- Or to **believe** that He will do what He says?

THINK SPOT

PRAY Ask God to help you to understand and believe His promises.

DAY 19

GARDENER'S QUESTION TIME

 Change **cry** to **joy** by changing just one letter at a time. *Try* hard (BIG clue!) *Answers at the bottom of the page.*

```
c r y
_ _ _
_ _ _
j o y
```

Mary M still thinks grave robbers have taken Jesus' body. She also thinks the tomb is empty—but when she looks inside she sees...

READ
John 20v10-13

What did Mary see?   Two a_____

But the angels aren't the only ones there...

READ
John 20v14-18

When Mary sees Jesus, who does she think He is? (v15)

The g_____

What does Jesus say to her? (v16)

As soon as Mary heard her name, she **knew** it was Jesus. How do you think she felt?

Circle your answers and add more of your own.

disappointed

puzzled

joyful

amazed

Cross out the **wrong** words below:

At first:
Mary is crying/joyful. She thinks/knows Jesus is dead/alive.

But now:
Mary is crying/joyful. She thinks/knows Jesus is dead/alive.

THINK + PRAY

Mary joyfully told the disciples that Jesus was alive. Who can **you** tell about Jesus this week? _____ Ask God to help you to tell your friends about Jesus.

DAY 20   # MEET JESUS!

John 20v19-23

Spot the difference. There are eight to find.

The disciples were together in a locked room—when **suddenly** they weren't alone any more...

READ
John 20v19-23

WOW!   Jesus really was there—even though the door was still locked!

What did Jesus show them? (v20)

> His h_____ and
> His s_____

What did Jesus tell them? (v21)

> As the F_____ sent
> me, I s_____ you.

Jesus was sending them to tell others about Him. Check out **God's Rescue Plan** (after Day 14) to remind you how Jesus came to forgive sins.

THINK SPOT

The disciples' job was to tell other people about Jesus the Rescuer.

- Have **you** been rescued by Jesus?
- Do you want to be? (Go back to **God's Rescue Plan** if you're not sure.)
- Do you want to tell your friends about Jesus?

PRAY   **Talk to Jesus about your answers. Ask Him to help you.**

DAY 21 THE MISSING DISCIPLE

When Jesus met His disciples in the locked room, one of them was missing! **Thomas** wasn't there. He refused to believe that Jesus was alive again—unless he could see and touch Jesus for himself.

READ
John 20v24-29

Thomas had to wait a whole week before seeing Jesus. But when he did see Jesus —he **believed**.

READ
John 20v30-31

This is where we started **Summer Signposts**. Why did John write his book?

John's aim is that we should believe that Jesus is our Lord and God—just as Thomas did. **Do you?**

PRAY

Father God, thank you for bringing Jesus back to life. Thank you that He is still alive today. Please help me to follow Him always as my Lord and God. Amen

What did Thomas say to Jesus?
Take the first letter of each picture to find the answer.

__ __ __ __ __ __ and __ __ __ __

WELCOME TO TABLE TALK

The aim of this section is to help you to read the Bible together as a family. Each day provides a short family Bible time which, with your own adaptation, could work for ages 4 to 10. We've included some optional follow on material linked with the XTB children's notes, which take the passage further for 7-10s.

TABLE TALK

A short family Bible time for daily use. Table Talk takes about five minutes, maybe at breakfast, or after an evening meal. Choose whatever time and place suits you best as a family.

Table Talk includes a simple discussion starter or activity that leads into a short Bible reading. This is followed by a few questions and a suggestion for prayer.

Table Talk can be used on its own, or alongside the XTB children's notes.

BUILDING UP

The Building Up section of Table Talk is designed to link up with XTB children's notes. After your child has worked through XTB on their own, the questions in Building Up can be used to build on what they have learned. Questions may reinforce the main teaching point, stretch your child's understanding or develop how the passage applies to us today.

Building Up can also be used as an extra question section to add to those in Table Talk. This may be particularly valuable if you have older children.

xtb XTB Bible-reading notes for children are based on the same passages from John as Table Talk. XTB notes can be used on their own, or with Table Talk.

Suggestions for using XTB and Table Talk:

★ The family do Table Talk together at breakfast. Older children do XTB on their own later, then share what they've learned with a parent using Building Up.
★ Or: Children use XTB notes on their own.
★ Or: Children's leaders use XTB and Table Talk to read the Bible with their group.
★ Or: Some or all of the family use Table Talk as the basis for a short family time, with added questions from the Building Up section when appropriate.

MAGNIFYING GLASS

Summer Signposts comes with a free magnifying glass. This is used in a number of activities during **XTB**—and also in **Table Talk**. You will find a picture of the XTB magnifying glass in the top corner of each Table Talk page. There is a miniature picture hidden inside each one. These pictures are all linked with the theme for the day. You may like to either start or finish each Table Talk session by asking your child to check the picture.

SIGNPOSTS

In John's Gospel we will look at seven of Jesus' miracles, which John says are like signposts, pointing to who Jesus is. However, these are not the only signs in the Bible. In the book of Romans, Paul says that all of Creation acts like a signpost pointing to God as our Creator.

> Ever since God created the world, his invisible qualities, both his eternal power and his divine nature, have been clearly seen; they are perceived in the things that God has made.
> Romans 1v20

An additional way you could use your magnifying glass would be to start each Table Talk session by using it to look closely at something God has created. (eg: your hand, fingernail, daisy, potato, rose petal, pebble, grass, orange, caterpillar...) Then remind each other that we come to *know* God, our Creator, by reading His word, the Bible. You could use a prayer like this:

Father God, thank you that You made everything in our world, and that You made and love us. Please help us now to understand what You are saying to us in the Bible. Amen

---

Today's passages are:
Table Talk: John 20v30-31
XTB: John 20v30-31

TABLE TALK

Talk about signposts. (Can you see any through the window?) What kinds of signpost can you think of? (Road names, warnings, school signs...) **Why** do we have signs?

READ

Signs often tell us things we need to know. John wrote his book because people need to know about Jesus.
Read John 20v30-31

TALK

What are the two reasons John gives for writing his book? (1—so we may believe in Jesus; 2—so that by believing we may have everlasting life with God.) John is saying that miracles are like **signposts**. They point to **who** Jesus is.

DO

(Optional) Find the mini signpost on Day 1 of **XTB**. Use the magnifying glass to read what it says.

PRAY

Ask God to help you to learn more about Jesus as you read John's book.

BUILDING UP

Today's **XTB** notes show that John wrote his book to point us to who Jesus is and why He came.

Ask your child what miracles are like. (*Signposts*) Ask them to show you the mini signpost and read what it says. Look up **John 21v25** together. Why didn't John write about **everything** that Jesus did?

DAY 2 WINE SIGN

Today's passages are:
Table Talk : John 2v7-11
XTB : John 2v1-11

TABLE TALK

DO
(You need pencil and paper.) Draw (or make!) a signpost with "Who Jesus is" written on it. Put it somewhere you'll see it whenever you do Table Talk together.

Note: If five verses is too long for your child then summarise the story and just read verse 11.

READ
Jesus, His mother Mary, and His disciples were at a wedding. When the wine ran out, Mary asked Jesus to help. Jesus told the servants to fill six huge jars with water. **Read John 2v7-11**

TALK
What did the servants put into the jars? (water) What was the water changed into? (wine) Who changed the water into wine? (Jesus) What did the disciples do? (v11—believed in Jesus)

THINK
The disciples didn't understand everything about who Jesus was—but they DID believe in Him, and followed Him. What do **you** believe about Jesus? What difference does this make to what you do?

Ask God to help you to understand more about Jesus, and how amazing He is.

PRAY

BUILDING UP

XTB looks at how Jesus' first miracle led to His disciples believing in Him.

Ask your child to tell you what Jesus' first miracle was. Talk about the disciples' belief in Jesus. What do you think they believed—and why? What do you believe about Jesus? Why?

DAY 3 THE ONE O'CLOCK MIRACLE

Today's passages are:
Table Talk : John 4v49-53
XTB : John 4v46-54

TABLE TALK

Talk about a time when your child was ill. How did they feel? How did mum or dad feel?

READ
In today's story, a boy is ill. His dad is very worried, and has walked 20 miles to see Jesus. He finds Jesus at one o'clock in the afternoon ("the seventh hour") —but Jesus doesn't come with him!
Read John 4v49-50

TALK
What did Jesus tell the man to do? (Go home.) Imagine the man walking 20 miles home again. It would take all night. How would he feel? What would he think about?

READ
The next day, when the man was nearly home, his servants rushed out to meet him. **Read John 4v51-53**

TALK
What time had the boy got better? (One o'clock—when Jesus was talking to his dad.) How did the man and his family react? (They believed in Jesus) Verse 50 describes faith as "taking Jesus at His word". Is this easy or hard? What can help you?

PRAY
Ask God to help you to believe His words to you in the Bible.

BUILDING UP

Read the **Think + Pray** box on the **XTB** page together. How did your child answer the question in the box? **XTB** says that "faith is a gift from God". Why do you think we need God's help to believe what He says?

TABLE TALK

Do you know anyone who uses a wheelchair? What things can't you do if you can't use your legs? What would you miss most?

READ

There was a pool in Jerusalem where ill people waited every day. They believed the water could cure them—but **only** if it started to bubble—and **only** the first person to get in! One day Jesus went there, and spoke to a man who'd not been able to walk for 38 years.
Read John 5v6-9

TALK

What did Jesus ask the man? (v6) At first, the man gave a silly, grumbly answer. But what did Jesus say next? (v8) How quickly was the man healed? (At once.) The man obeyed Jesus—and was healed. Think of times when obeying Jesus is hard or seems silly. (Adults must be honest here too. See **Building Up** for examples.)

PRAY

The Bible tells us that obeying Jesus is **always** the best thing to do. Ask Jesus to help you to obey Him, even when it's hard.

BUILDING UP

Ask your child to tell you the story—what did Jesus do, who was healed, who was cross about it?

Talk about times when obeying Jesus is hard. (eg: owning up when we've done wrong, not joining in with friends who gossip, being kind to those we don't like.) Do they believe that obeying Jesus is **always** best? Why / why not?

TABLE TALK

Remind each other of yesterday's miracle. What are the miracles like? (Signposts) What do they point to? (Who Jesus is.)

READ

This miracle pointed to who Jesus was—but some people completely missed the point! **Read John 5v9-10**

TALK

What day of the week was it? (The Sabbath—God's special day of rest) The Jewish leaders had made rules about the Sabbath. One was "You mustn't carry anything." How did the healed man break their rule? (By carrying his mat.)

THINK

What did the **Jewish leaders** think was the most important thing about this story? What do **you** think is the most important thing about this story? (Clue: what does the signpost show?)

PRAY

Ask God to help you not to miss the point about Jesus as you read about Him.

BUILDING UP

Today's **XTB** notes look at how the man obeyed Jesus, but the Jewish leaders hated Him. In John's book we see different reactions to Jesus—love, hate, surprise, obedience, learning, puzzled... Are any of these true for **your child**? Which are true for **you**? Pray together about your answers.

DAY 6 FISHY BUSINESS

Today's passages are:
Table Talk : John 6v8-13
XTB : John 6v5-13

TABLE TALK

Either: If you're eating a meal, share just **one** person's food among all of you! Did you all have enough to eat? Why/why not? *Or:* Read "Counting Up" in **Notes for Parents**. Use this method to count the people in your family, your class at school, at work... (ie: **don't** count women or children!)

READ
In today's story, one boy's packed lunch was shared between thousands of people—and it was enough!
Read John 6v8-13

TALK
How many **men** were there? (5000—but see "Counting Up" in **Notes for Parents**.) How many small loaves did the boy have? (5) How many fish? (2) Is this enough to feed thousands of people? (No!) So **why** was it enough this time?

THINK
"Jesus can meet all our needs—and more!" Talk about how that makes you feel. (*Note:* This **doesn't** mean Jesus will give us everything we want. Why not?)

PRAY
Ask Jesus to help you to trust Him to meet all your needs.

BUILDING UP

Today's **XTB** notes show that "even the biggest problem is NO PROBLEM for Jesus."

Ask your child to tell you the story. Why couldn't the disciples feed the crowd? (v7) Why could **Jesus** feed them? Does your child believe that Jesus can help with **any** problem? Do **you**? Does that mean He will answer straight away? Will He always give us what we ask? Why / why not?

COUNTING UP

When they counted groups of people in Bible times, they only counted men—and boys aged 12 or over. (Boys were thought of as men once they were 12.) They didn't count women, girls or boys under 12 at all! Jesus fed 5000 **men**—plus women and children. Probably over 15,000 in all!

OLD TESTAMENT LINKS

The Feeding of the 5000 has very strong links with a key event in the Old Testament. After God had used Moses to rescue the Israelites from Egypt, they spent 40 years wandering through the desert. During that time there was no food for them, so God provided food miraculously—flocks of quail and something called manna (which tasted like biscuits made with honey). You can read about these events in **Exodus 16v1-18.**

In the desert, God miraculously provided food for huge numbers of people. 1500 years later Jesus did the same thing—and the crowds recognised the similarity. Older children might like to find out about this story for themselves, and see if they can spot the similarities with Jesus' miracle.

God had promised to send a prophet (God's messenger) like Moses. (*This promise is in Deuteronomy 18v15.*) This is "the Prophet" the crowds refer to in John 6v14. Moses had rescued the Israelites from slavery in Egypt—so the people thought this new Prophet would rescue them too—from the Roman occupation.

When the people saw Jesus' miracle, they thought He had come to free them from the Romans. That's why they tried to make Him their king (John 6v15). (*Note:* They were partly correct—Jesus *had* come as King—but to bring a completely different kind of rescue, as we'll see on Day 14.)

Today's passages are:
Table Talk : John 6v14-15
XTB : John 6v14-15

TABLE TALK

Note: Read **Notes for Parents** to see the Old Testament background to this miracle.

At the time of Jesus, the Romans had taken over Israel. What would it be like to live in an occupied country, with a conquering army making the rules? How would you feel about the Romans?

God had promised to send a prophet (God's messenger) like Moses—and a King, who would rescue His people. **Read John 6v14-15**

READ

Who did the crowds say Jesus was? (The promised Prophet) What did they want Jesus to become? (King) But what did Jesus do? (He left.)

TALK

Jesus **is** King—but not the kind the crowds expected. Christians follow Jesus as King. What do you think it means for Jesus to be King of your life? (He's in charge of your life, He looks after you, you need to obey Him...)

THINK

Ask God to help you to obey Jesus as King, even when it's hard.

PRAY

BUILDING UP

Today's **XTB** notes show that the crowds wanted King Jesus to rescue them from the Romans, but that Jesus really came as King of our lives.

Ask your child what kind of king the crowds wanted Jesus to be. Ask what they think it means to have Jesus as **their** King. Are **they** following King Jesus? Are **you**?

Today's passages are:
Table Talk: John 6v19-21
XTB: John 6v16-21

TABLE TALK

Talk about the things that scare you. (Spiders? The dark? Thunder?) In today's story the disciples are alone in a small boat, in the dark, in a bad storm. What do you think they'll be most scared of?

As we'll see, it's not the storm that frightens the disciples—it's Jesus!
Read John 6v19-21

READ

How did Jesus reach the disciples? (He walked on the water!) How did they feel? (Terrified) What did Jesus say to them? (See v20.) This miracle is another signpost. What does it point to? (Who Jesus is.)

TALK

(Optional) **Read John 20v31** again to remind you what the miracles show about who Jesus is.

DO

Look up Day 8 in **XTB**. Read the "Did You Know?" box together. Think about **who** Jesus is. Why should that help you not to be afraid?

THINK

Dear Jesus, thank you that You are **always** able to help us—and You **never** let us down.

PRAY

BUILDING UP

See if you can remember the five miracles John has written about. Use the magnifying glass to check your answers on the **XTB** page. Look up John 20v31 together. How does this fifth miracle show that Jesus is the Son of God?

DAY 9   SIGHT FOR SORE EYES

Today's passages are:
Table Talk : John 9v6-9
       XTB : John 9v6-25

TABLE TALK

Note: *Please read the whole of chapter 9 beforehand, so that you can sum up the story for your child. They might even like to act it out.*

Use the magnifying glass to look closely at something small (a rice crispie? a pin? a seeds?)

READ The man in today's story couldn't look at anything at all—he was born blind. **Read John 9v6-9**

TALK What did Jesus put on the man's eyes? What did Jesus say to him? (v7) What happened as the man washed his face?

THINK People who knew the man argued about him. They could **see** the man—but some didn't **believe** what they were seeing! Later, the Jewish leaders even called his parents in to check he really was their son! (v18-23) Why do you think it was hard to believe what they were seeing? Many people **saw** the miracles, but didn't **believe** that Jesus was the Son of God. Why do you think that was?

PRAY We need God's help to see who Jesus really is. Ask God to help you to see and understand who Jesus is as you read the Bible together.

BUILDING UP

Ask your child to tell you the story. Read the **Think + Pray** box together. Who did your child say they would tell about Jesus this week? Who can **you** tell about Jesus this week? Pray for each other, asking God to help you.

DAY 10   WHAT AN EYE-OPENER!

Today's passages are:
Table Talk : John 9v35-38
       XTB : John 9v35-38

TABLE TALK

Recap the story from yesterday. How did Jesus heal the blind man? How did people react?

READ As you read the verses, look out for two names for Jesus. **Read John 9v35-38**

TALK What was the **first** name given for Jesus? (v35, Son of Man—this title is used in Daniel 7v13-14 to refer to the Messiah (Christ)—Jesus often used it to refer to Himself.) What was the **second** name for Jesus? (Lord, v38) Look back to v11 to see what this man first called Jesus. ("The man called Jesus")

This man's spiritual eyes have been opened—he now sees **who** Jesus is and believes in Him. *(Remember—this is what the miracles point to.)* Talk about ways each of you has come to see Jesus more clearly. *(This may be a good time for an adult to explain how they became a Christian, and why.)*

PRAY Thank God for opening your eyes so that you can see who Jesus is.

BUILDING UP

Ask your child to tell you the answers to the **XTB** arrow code. Why do they think this man's understanding of Jesus grew? Talk about whether they (& you!) really want to get to know Jesus better too. Why/why not? Pray together about your answers.

THE DEATH OF LAZARUS

Table Talk and XTB both spend three days looking at this story. You will find it helpful to read the whole of chapter 11 first so that you're familiar with it.

TALKING ABOUT DEATH WITH CHILDREN

Children may have loads of questions about death and heaven. One four-year-old friend of mine asked his Mummy last week: "Do people sleep in heaven?" The Bible tells us that Jesus has prepared a special place for us in heaven:

> In my Father's house are many rooms; if it were not so I would have told you. I am going there to prepare a place for you.
> John 14v2

We can assure children that heaven will be the **best** it can possibly be. But the Bible doesn't really tell us much about it—we will have to wait and see. So it's OK not to know the answers to all their questions!

Talking to children about death can be tricky. It so depends on what kind of question they ask, and **why** they are asking. Your local Christian bookshop will stock a range of booklets designed to help children think about death. You may find some of these helpful. Or ask other Christian parents how they have answered similar questions.

As we look at the death and resurrection of Lazarus, there will be opportunities to explain the Christian view of death, and the **certainty** we can have if we are followers of Jesus. Be sure that your children understand that being with Jesus in heaven will be wonderful, and is a **sure** promise for all those who have put their trust in Him.

DAY 11 DYING TO SEE YOU

Today's passages are:
Table Talk: John 11v3-6
XTB: John 11v1-6

TABLE TALK

Turn to Day 11 of **XTB**. Read the cartoon together. How do you think Joe felt at first? How did he feel when he found his friends has something better planned?

READ Lazarus, and his sisters Mary and Martha, were Jesus' friends. When Lazarus became very ill, his sisters sent Jesus a message. **Read John 11v3-6**

TALK Did Jesus go to see Lazarus straight away? (No!) How long did Jesus wait? (2 days) Jesus said this had happened so that someone would be glorified (v4). Who? (God **and** God's Son—Jesus) This was going to be another signpost pointing to who Jesus is—but the disciples had to **wait** to see how.

THINK **Could** Jesus have healed Lazarus? (YES!) But He didn't—because He had something better planned. **Could** God answer all our prayers? (YES!)

But sometimes He says No, or He asks us to wait, because He has something better planned.

It can be hard to trust that God always does what's best. Ask Him to help you.

PRAY

BUILDING UP

Ask your child to tell you the story. What surprised them about this story? Jesus said it was **good** that He hadn't been with Lazarus. Read John 11v14-15 to see why. Talk about times when it feels like God is ignoring your prayers. How can you help each other to wait for God's answer?

DAY 12   LIFE OR DEATH

Today's passages are:
Table Talk: John 11v25-27
XTB: John 11v17-27

TABLE TALK

Recap yesterday's story. Who was dying? (Lazarus) Who sent the message to Jesus? (Mary and Martha) How long did Jesus wait? (2 days)

READ By the time Jesus arrived, Lazarus had been dead for **four days**. Jesus was about to do an amazing miracle. But first He had something very important to say to Martha (and to us!) **Read John 11v25-27**

TALK Jesus said that anyone "who believes in Him will live, even though he dies" (v25) What do you think He meant? (Life on earth **ends**. Our body dies—we don't need it any more. Life in heaven with Jesus **never ends!** We will have new bodies—and never be ill or in pain. This is a promise for everyone who believes in Jesus—and Jesus **always** keeps His promises!

THINK Sometimes people worry about death. Why do Jesus' words help us not to be scared of dying? (See *Notes for Parents* for help on talking with children about death)

PRAY Thank Jesus that you can look forward to a wonderful home in heaven with Him.

BUILDING UP

Today's **XTB** notes show that Jesus "is the resurrection and the life".

Ask your child what they think this means. See **Notes for Parents** on the previous page for help on how to talk with your child about death and heaven.

DAY 13   DEAD OR ALIVE?

Today's passages are:
Table Talk: John 11v43-44
XTB: John 11v32-45

TABLE TALK

Think back to Day 11. How long did Jesus wait? (2 days) Jesus didn't rush to cure Lazarus because He had something better planned. Do you know (or can you guess) what it was?

READ Lazarus was buried in a cave-sealed with a huge stone. Jesus had the stone moved away. He prayed to God His Father—and then He spoke to Lazarus! **Read John 11v43-44**

TALK When Jesus told Lazarus to come out of the tomb, what happened? (He did!) Dead bodies were usually wrapped in strips of cloth before burial, so what did Jesus tell the people to do? (Unwrap him.) What do Jesus' miracles point to? (Who Jesus is.) So why do you think Jesus could do this amazing miracle? (Because of who He is.)

THINK John tells us in v45 that many people believed in Jesus after seeing this miracle. What about **you**? Have you all put your faith in Jesus? (If you're not sure, tomorrow's Table Talk will help you.)

PRAY You've read about seven miracles in Jesus' book. Thank God that these help you to see clearly who Jesus is.

BUILDING UP

Ask your child to tell you the whole story, from Lazarus first being ill until Jesus brought him back to life. What does this story show about Jesus? (He always does what's best, He has power over death, He is the Son of God...)

Today's passages are:
Table Talk: John 3v16
XTB: John 3v16

TABLE TALK

DO

(You need pencil and paper.) Take turns
to draw a picture clue for one of Jesus'
seven miracles. The others guess which
miracle it is. (Day 14 of **XTB** has a list.)

These miracles are like seven signposts.
They point to **who** Jesus is. Now we're
going to find out **why** Jesus came.

READ

Read John 3v16

TALK

Who sent Jesus into the world? (God)
Why did God send Jesus? (Because He
loved us, so that those who believe in
Jesus may have eternal life.)

DO

Copy this verse onto a large sheet of
paper. Put it next to your picture or
model of a signpost (from Day 2).

Family Challenge: This is the most famous
verse in the Bible. Why not learn it! (eg: you
could sing it to a nursery rhyme—Old King
Cole?—or maybe even rap it!)

PRAY

Thank God for loving you so much
that He sent Jesus to die for you.

BUILDING UP

Today's **XTB** notes show that
God sent Jesus to be our Rescuer
because He loves us.

Read **God's Rescue Plan** together
(after Day 14 of XTB). Together,
think of one sentence to sum
up why Jesus came.

Today's passages are:
Table Talk : John 19v25-27
XTB : John 19v23-27

TABLE TALK

Recap: Jesus' miracles were signposts
pointing to who He is. But Jesus' enemies
didn't like what they saw. Their **WICKED PLOT**
was to have Him arrested and killed.

Jesus was handed over to the
Romans—who crucified Him. He was
nailed to a cross and left to die.

READ

Read John 19v25-27

TALK

Who stood near the cross? (v25)
Jesus spoke to His mother, and to
John ("the disciple Jesus loved").
What did Jesus say to Mary? (Here is
your son.) What did He say to John? (Here
is your mother.) John was to care for Mary
like a son.

THINK

We saw yesterday that God's
WONDERFUL PLAN is all about LOVE.
God loves us—so He sent Jesus to be
our Rescuer. **Jesus loves us**—so He
chose to die on the cross for us. Jesus **loved**
Mary too—so He made sure she was cared
for. As Jesus' followers we should be like
Him—**loving** and caring for others, however
we feel.

PRAY

Think of a practical way to show
someone you love them this
week. Ask God to help you.

BUILDING UP

Ask your child to explain the
Wicked Plot and the **Wonderful Plan**.
Both of these plans meant that Jesus would
die. Why did Jesus' enemies want Him to
die? (They hated Him.) What's the **real** reason for
Jesus' death? (He died as our Rescuer.)

DAY 16 ALL FINISHED

Today's passages are:
Table Talk: John 19v28-30
XTB: John 19v28-30

TABLE TALK

DO (You need pencil and paper.) Write "I've finished!" in a speech bubble. Think of times you might say this. (eg: finished... a jigsaw, the washing up, your homework, running a marathon...)

READ In today's reading, Jesus finishes what He came to do.
Read John 19v28-30

TALK Why did Jesus ask for a drink? (v28) (So that Scripture would come true—Jesus was completing the Rescue Plan God spoke about in the Old Testament.) What did Jesus say just before He died? (v30) (It is finished.) What had Jesus finished? (His job as our Rescuer.)

THINK Jesus died on a Friday. Why do we call it **Good** Friday? (Jesus did a **good** thing when He rescued us.)

PRAY Thank God for sending Jesus to rescue you.

BUILDING UP

Today's **XTB** notes show that Jesus had finished His job as our Rescuer.

Ask your child what two things Jesus said just before He died. Why did He say these things? Jesus died to rescue us from our sins. Did He have to do anything else to rescue us? (No!—His job as Rescuer was finished.)

DAY 17 THE END OF THE ROAD?

Today's passages are:
Table Talk : John 19v40-42
XTB : John 19v38-42

TABLE TALK

Recap: What day of the week did Jesus die? (Friday) Why do we call it **Good** Friday? (Jesus did a **good** thing when He died for us.)

READ After Jesus died, two of His followers—Joseph and Nicodemus—asked the Romans if they could have the body. Then they buried Jesus.
Read John 19v40-42

TALK What did Jesus' friends put on the body? (Spices, then wrapped it in strips of linen cloth.) Where was Jesus buried? (A new tomb, in a garden) How do you think they felt as they buried Jesus?

THINK It looked like the Wicked Plot to murder Jesus had won. But God was always in charge. The Bible says God is always in control—even when it doesn't look or feel like it. Do you believe this? How can you help each other to keep trusting God? (eg: remember God's promises, remind each other how God has answered your prayers, pray together...)

PRAY Ask God to help you to trust Him, even when things seem out of control.

BUILDING UP

XTB today looks at Jesus' burial. Ask your child to tell you about Jesus' burial. Who buried Him? How and where? *XTB* asks "Is this the end of the road?" Is it? Why / why not?

Today's passages are:
Table Talk: John 20v6-8
XTB: John 20v1-9

TABLE TALK

If you had a short race (eg: to the end of the garden)—who would win? (Do it—if you can!)

READ It's now Sunday morning. Mary M has just told Peter and John that Jesus' body is missing from the tomb! They race up the hill to see. John is the fastest—he gets there first. But when Peter arrives, he goes right inside the tomb. **Read John 20v6-8**

TALK What did Peter see in the tomb? (The cloth that had been wrapped round Jesus' body.) Was Jesus' body in the tomb? (No!) When John followed Peter into the tomb, what did he do? (He saw—and believed.)

The Old Testament said Jesus would come back to life again. Jesus had said so as well—but His friends hadn't understood. (**Optional**—read Jesus' words in Luke 18v31-34.) Do you sometimes find it hard to understand or believe what God says in the Bible. What can help?

PRAY Ask God to help you understand and believe what He says in the Bible.

BUILDING UP

Today's **XTB** looks at the events of Easter Sunday morning. Ask your child to tell you the story. What two reasons were there for expecting Jesus to come back to life? (*The Scriptures/Old Testament said so, and so did Jesus Himself.*) Verse 8 says John "saw and believed". What do you think he believed?

Today's passages are:
Table Talk : John 20v10-18
XTB : John 20v10-18

TABLE TALK

Guess the Geezer: Take it in turns to think of someone you all know. Give clues until the others guess who you're thinking of.

READ Jesus' tomb is empty—the body is missing. Mary M thinks grave robbers have taken the body—but she's about to have a huge surprise! First, she meets two angels! Then the gardener speaks to her. But is he really the gardener...? **Read John 20v10-18** (or just v14-16 if this is too long.)

TALK Who did Mary think Jesus was? (The gardener.) What did she ask Him? (Where the body was.) When did Mary realise that she was really with Jesus? (When He said her name.)

Once Mary knew that Jesus was alive, she rushed to tell the disciples (v18). Is there someone **you** can tell about Jesus this week? (Or invite them to church or to your Sunday group.) Pray for them, and ask God to help you tell them about Jesus.

PRAY

BUILDING UP

Ask your child to show you the puzzle changing CRY to JOY. Ask them why Mary M changed from crying to being full of joy. Who did Mary tell the good news to? (v18) Who can your child tell about Jesus this week? How can you help?

DAY 20 MEET JESUS!

LOOKING CLOSELY

Have a competition—who has the cleanest fingernails? Now use the magnifying glass. Are they **really** clean? Are they nibbled or chipped? Are they perfect?

When we look at our lives we may look OK. In fact some of us look pretty good! But God sees us close up. He sees every detail. No matter how good we look to ourselves, God sees when we're selfish, or tell lies, or don't help someone. God sees our **sin**.

What is Sin?

We all like to be in charge of our own lives. We do what **we** want instead of what **God** wants. This is called Sin.

Sin is a BIG problem. It gets in the way between us and God. It stops us from knowing God and stops us from being His friends. The final result of sin is death.

Read John 3v16 together. (You may have a poster of it from Day 14.)

GOD LOVES US! He loves us **so much** that He sent His own Son Jesus to rescue us from sin. Unlike us, Jesus is perfect. He **never** sinned. As Jesus died, all the sins of the world were put onto Him. He took all of our sin onto Himself, taking all the punishment we deserve.

That's why John 3v16 can promise us eternal life. Jesus died for us—so that we can be forgiven, and live with Jesus in heaven for ever.

(For a fuller explanation see God's Rescue Plan after Day 14 of XTB.)

Today's passages are:
Table Talk : John 20v19-21
XTB : John 20v19-23

TABLE TALK

Close the door and windows. Lock them if you can. On Easter Sunday evening the disciples met together in a locked room—because they were afraid. What do you think they were scared of? *(Remember what's just happened to Jesus.)*

READ — Suddenly, even though the door was locked, someone else was in the room with them! **Read John 20v19-21**

TALK — Who appeared in the room? (Jesus) What did Jesus show them? *(His hands and side—where the nails and spear had left scars, John 19v34)* What did Jesus tell them? (See v21)

THINK — Jesus sent His disciples to tell others about Him. They could tell people about the miracles—**so can you.** They could tell them about the events of Easter—**so can you.** They could point people to Jesus the Rescuer, who came to forgive sins. **Can you?** *("Looking Closely"—in Notes for Parents—will help you to be clear what sin is and why we need to be rescued from it.)*

PRAY — Thank God for bringing Jesus back to life again on Easter Sunday.

BUILDING UP

Ask your child to tell you what happened on the first Easter Sunday evening. What job did Jesus give to His disciples. List some of the things the disciples would be able to tell other people about Jesus. Jesus wants us to tell others about Him too. Why?

DAY 21 THE MISSING DISCIPLE

Today's passages are:
Table Talk: John 20v26-28
XTB: John 20v24-31

TABLE TALK

Think back over the amazing things you have read in John's Gospel. Which do you find most incredible? Why?

READ

Incredible—but true! His disciples had seen Him. But **one** was missing. Thomas wasn't there—and he refused to believe it unless he could see and touch Jesus for himself. **Read John 20v26-28**

Thomas had to wait a whole week—but what happened then? (Jesus appeared as before, but Thomas **was** there.) What did Jesus tell Thomas to do? (See v27) What did Thomas say to Jesus? ("My Lord and my God!")

DO

(Optional) **Read v30-31** together to remind you why John wrote his book.

John's aim is that we will believe that Jesus is **our Lord and God**—just as Thomas did. **Do you?**

PRAY

Ask Jesus to help you to follow Him as your Lord and God every day.

BUILDING UP

Ask your child what they have learnt about Jesus today in **XTB**. (*Jesus really is alive. He is Lord and God.*) What other things have they learnt about Jesus using **Summer Signposts**? Have a look at the **What Next** ideas opposite. What will they do next to find out more about Jesus?

WHAT NEXT?

Read some other stories written by John. These ones tell you about one of Jesus' closest friends, called Peter...

•Peter becomes a disciple   John 1v35-42
•Peter keeps following Jesus   John 6v60-71
•Jesus washes Peter's feet   John 13v1-14
•Jesus says Peter will deny Him   John 13v36-38
•Peter tries to save Jesus   John 18v1-14
•Peter denies Jesus   John 18v15-18 & 25-27
•Peter sees the empty tomb   John 20v1-10
•Peter has breakfast with Jesus   John 21v1-14
•Jesus forgives Peter   John 21v15-19

MORE XTB & TABLE TALK

There are twelve full issues of XTB, each with 65 full XTB pages, plus 26 days of extra readings. There are twelve issues of Table Talk based on the same readings and themes as XTB.

There are also two more seasonal editions of XTB:

- **Christmas Unpacked**
- **Easter Unscrambled**

All available from your local The Good Book Company website:
UK: www.thegoodbook.co.uk
N America: www.thegoodbook.com
Australia: www.thegoodbook.com.au
N Zealand: www.thegoodbook.co.nz